# EASY PIANO SELECTIONS FROM

T004091T

ALL FOR THE BEST _____ 13

ALL GOOD GIFTS_____ 19

BLESS THE LORD_____ 8

BY MY SIDE _____ 34

DAY BY DAY _____ 4

LEARN YOUR LESSONS WELL _____ 40

LIGHT OF THE WORLD_____ 46

ON THE WILLOWS _____ 42

PREPARE YE (THE WAY OF THE LORD) ___ 2

TURN BACK, O MAN _____ 28

WE BESEECH THEE _____ 23

Applications for performance of this work, whether legitimate, stock,
amateur, or foreign, should be addressed to:
THEATRE MAXIMUS
1650 Broadway
New York, NY 10019

ISBN 978-0-7935-6685-3

HAL•LEONARD®
CORPORATION
7777 W. BLUEMOUND RD. P.O. BOX 13819 MILWAUKEE, WI 53213

# PREPARE YE
## (The Way Of The Lord)

Words and Music by
STEPHEN SCHWARTZ

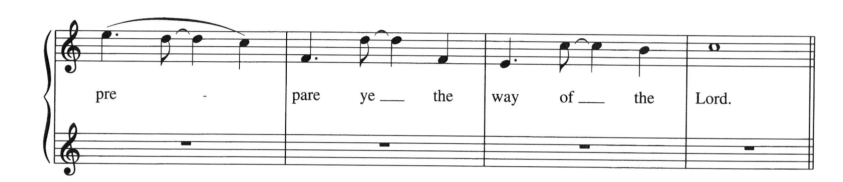

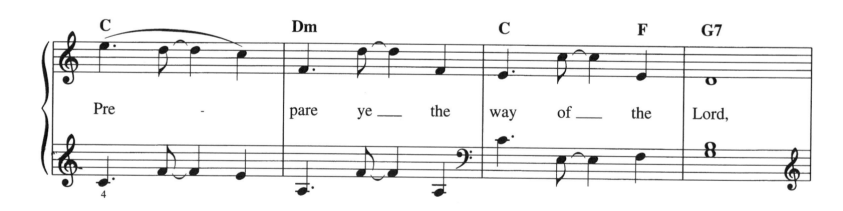

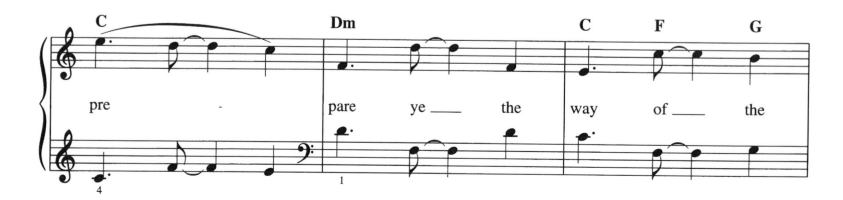

3

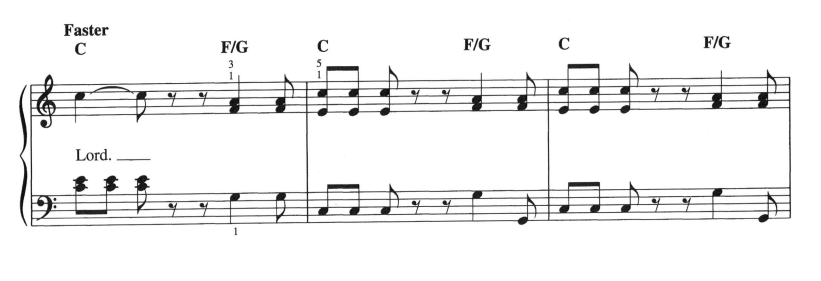

Lord. ____

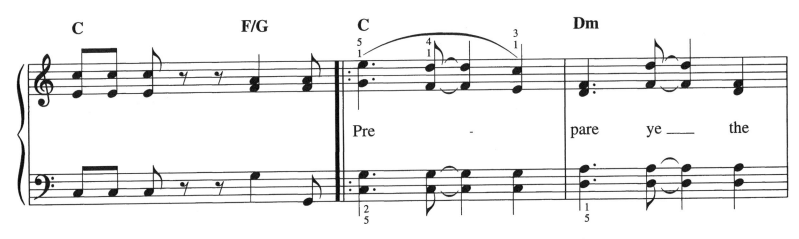

Pre - pare ye ____ the

way of ____ the Lord, pre -

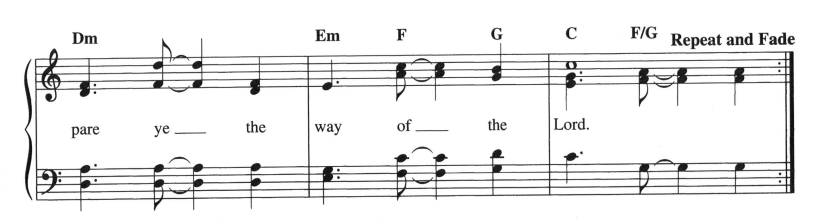

pare ye ____ the way of ____ the Lord.

# DAY BY DAY

Words and Music by
STEPHEN SCHWARTZ

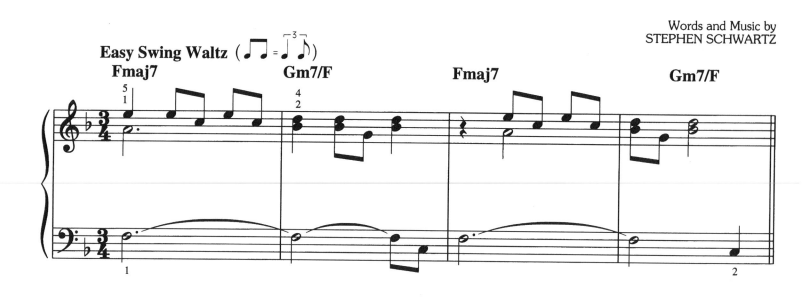

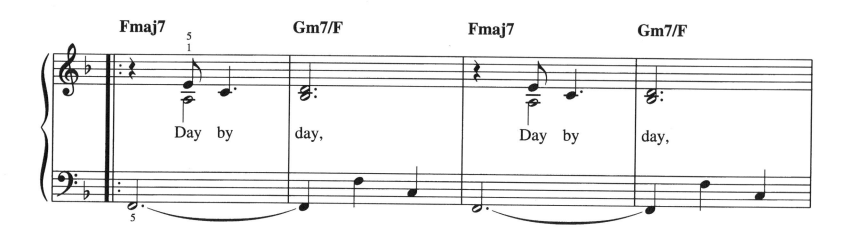

Day by day, Day by day,

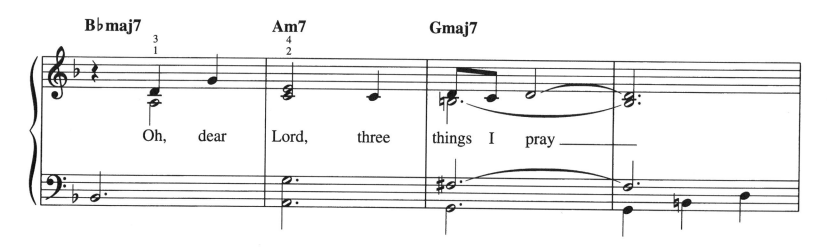

Oh, dear Lord, three things I pray

to see Thee more clear - ly, love Thee more

dear - ly, fol - low Thee more near - ly, _____

day by day. _____  day by day. _____

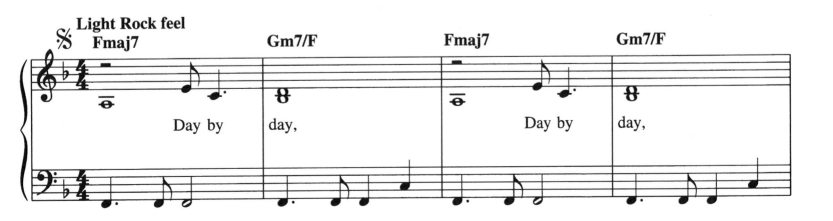

**Light Rock feel**

Day by day, Day by day,

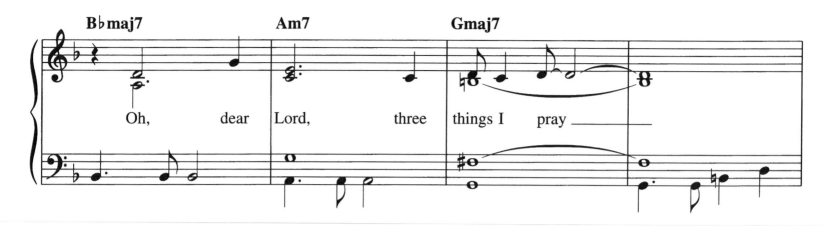

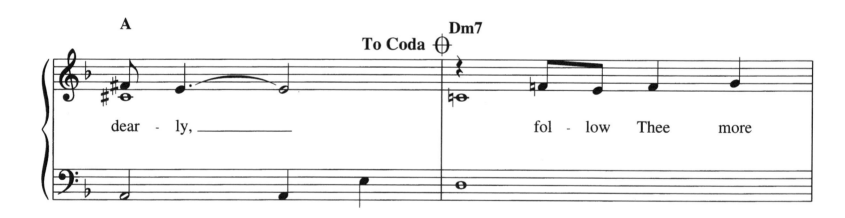

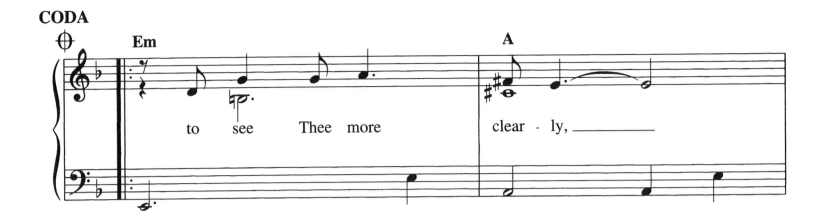

**CODA**

Em — to see Thee more — A — clear - ly, _____

Em7 — love Thee more — A — *Play 3 times* — dear - ly, _____ — Dm7 — fol - low Thee more

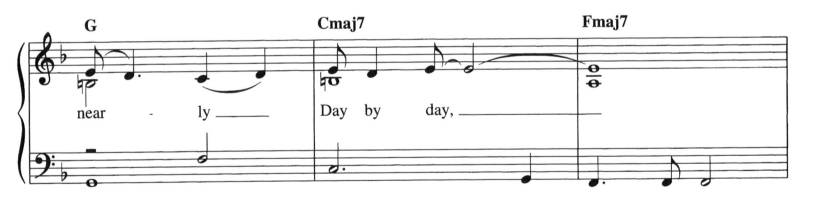

G — near - ly _____ — Cmaj7 — Day by day, _____ — Fmaj7

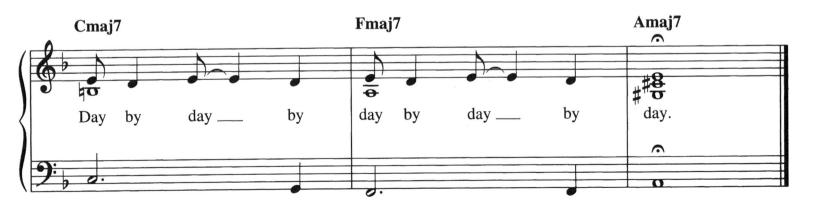

Cmaj7 — Day by day _____ by — Fmaj7 — day by day _____ by — Amaj7 — day.

# BLESS THE LORD

Words and Music by
STEPHEN SCHWARTZ

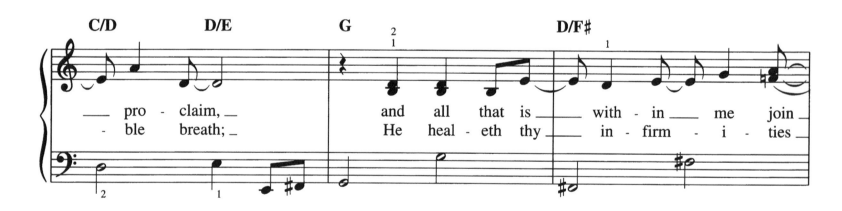

O bless the Lord, ___ my soul, ___ His mer - cies bear ___
He clothes thee with ___ His love, ___ up - holds thee with

___ in mind ___ for - get not all ___ His ben - e - fits,
___ His truth ___ and like the ea - gle He re - news ___

**Brighter tempo**

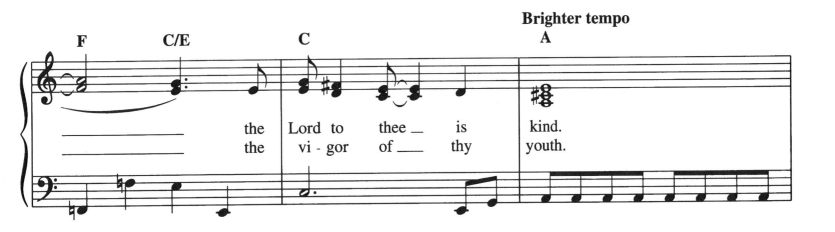

the Lord to thee ___ is kind.
the vi - gor of ___ thy youth.

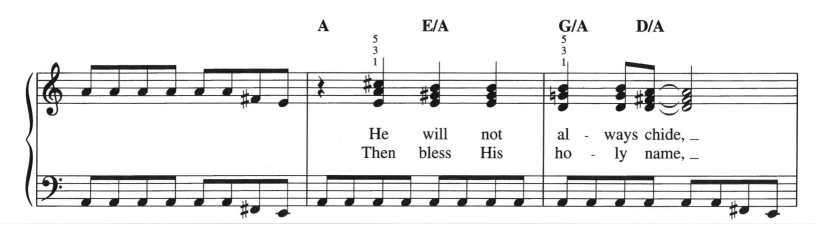

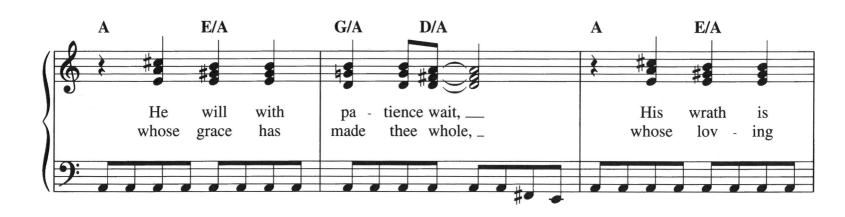

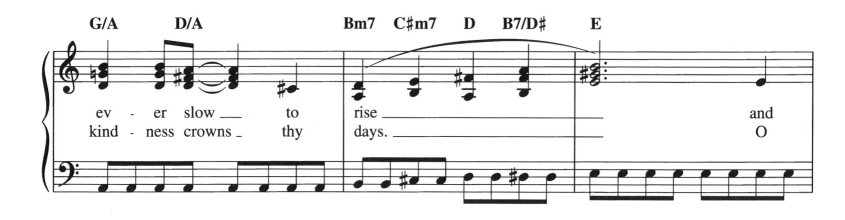

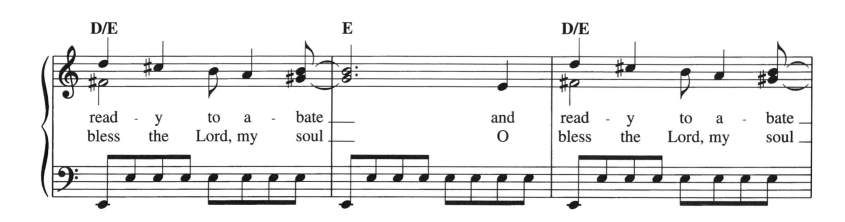

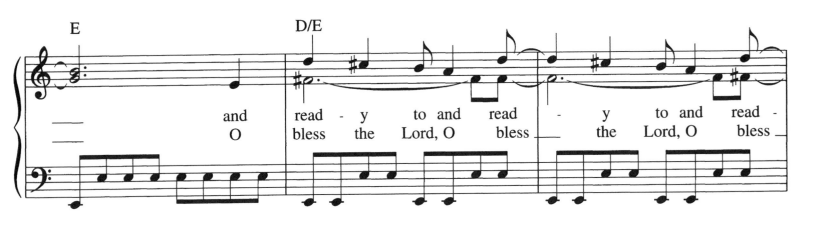

# ALL FOR THE BEST

Words and Music by
STEPHEN SCHWARTZ

**Freely**

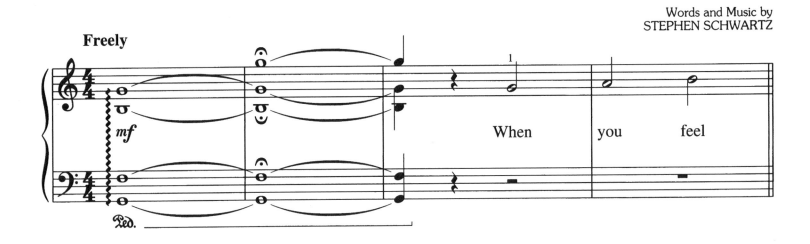

When you feel

**Soft Shoe tempo**

sad        or un - der a    curse,              your life is

bad,        your pros - pects are   worse,          your wife is

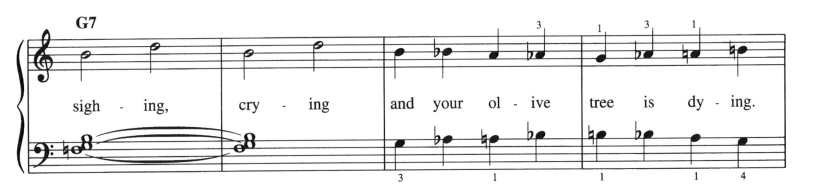

sigh - ing,      cry - ing    and your ol - ive   tree is   dy - ing.

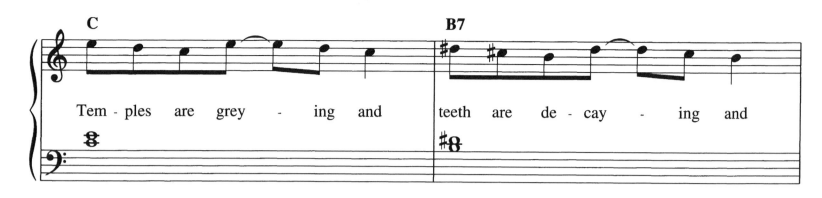

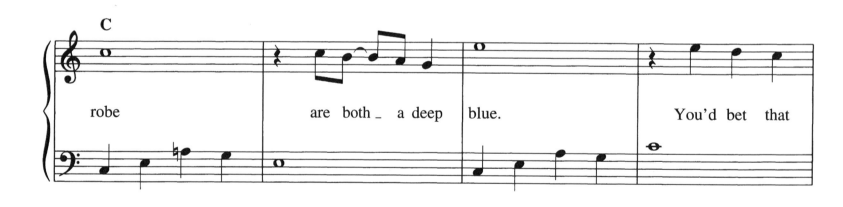

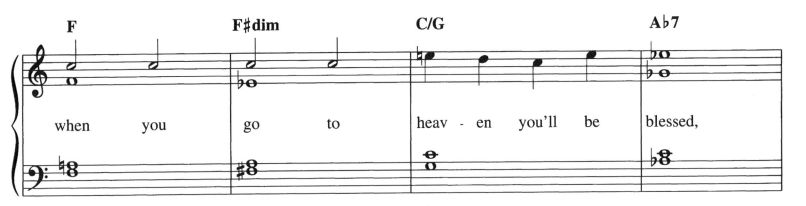

when you go to heav - en you'll be blessed,

**Very bright 2**

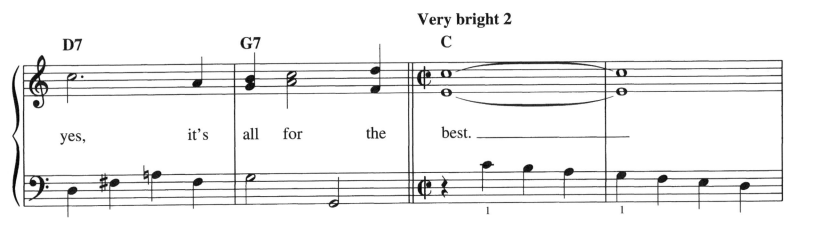

yes, it's all for the best. _____

Some men are born to live at ease, do - ing

what they please, rich - er than the bees are in hon - ey,

never grow-ing old, nev-er feel-ing cold, pull-ing pots of gold from the air.

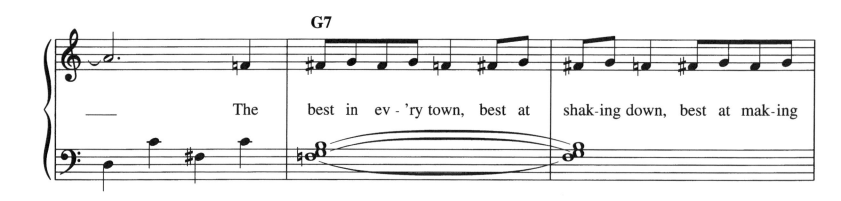

The best in ev-'ry town, best at shak-ing down, best at mak-ing

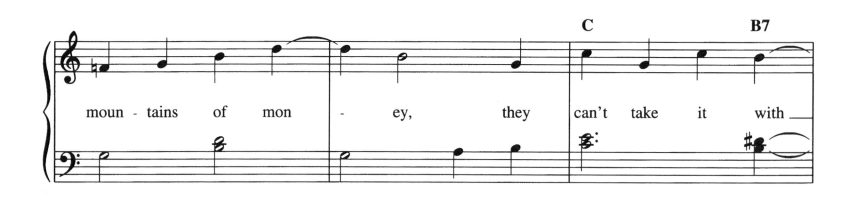

moun-tains of mon - ey, they can't take it with

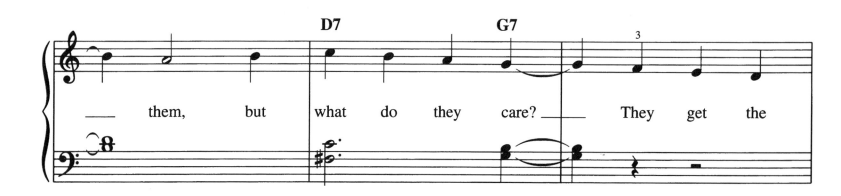

them, but what do they care? They get the

center of the meat, cush-ions on their seat, hous-es on a street where it's sun -

- ny. Sum-mers at the sea, win-ters warm and free, all of this and

we get the rest, \_\_\_\_\_ but, who is the land \_\_\_\_\_

for, the sun and the sand \_\_\_\_\_ for? You

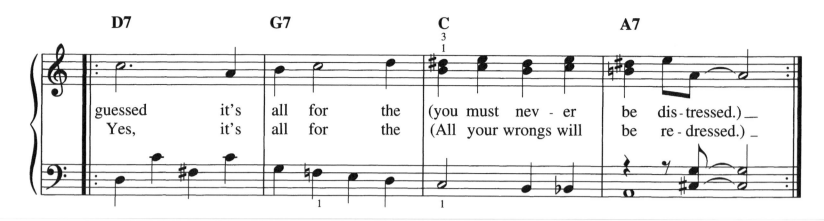

guessed it's all for the (you must nev - er be dis - tressed.) __
Yes, it's all for the (All your wrongs will be re - dressed.) __

Yes, it's all for the (Some-one's got to be op - pressed!) __

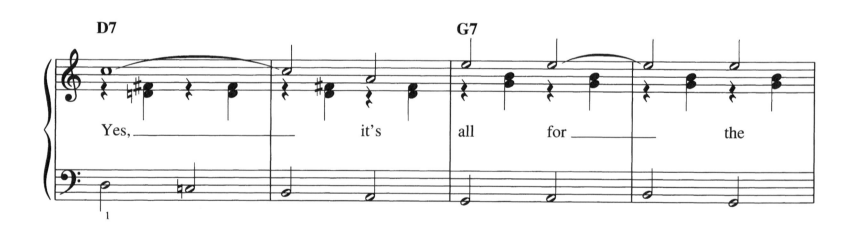

Yes, _____ it's all for _____ the

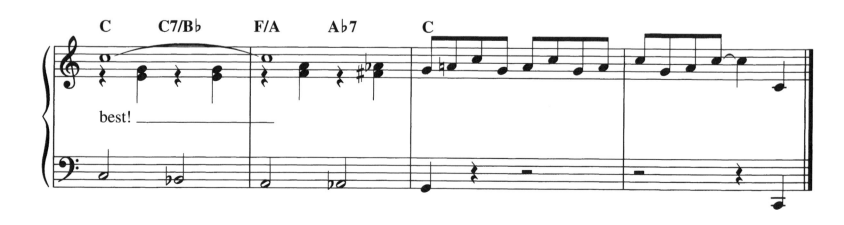

best! _____

# ALL GOOD GIFTS

Words and Music by
STEPHEN SCHWARTZ

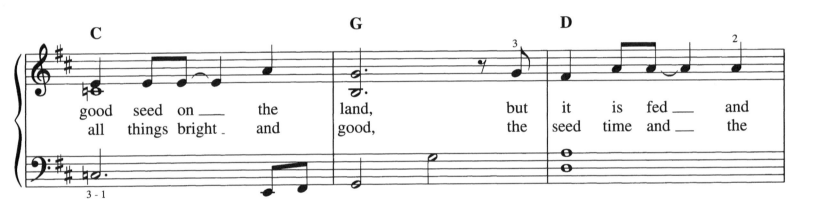

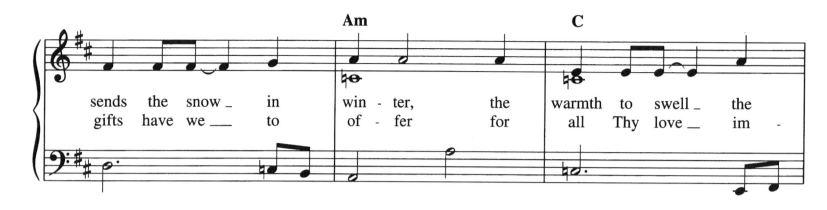

sends the snow _ in | win - ter, the | warmth to swell _ the
gifts have we _ to | of - fer for | all Thy love _ im -

grain, | the breez - es and _ the | sun - shine and
parts, but | that which Thou _ de - | sir - est and our

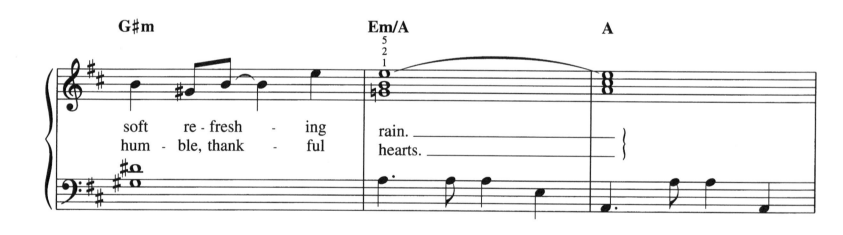

soft re - fresh - ing | rain. _____ |
hum - ble, thank - ful | hearts. _____ |

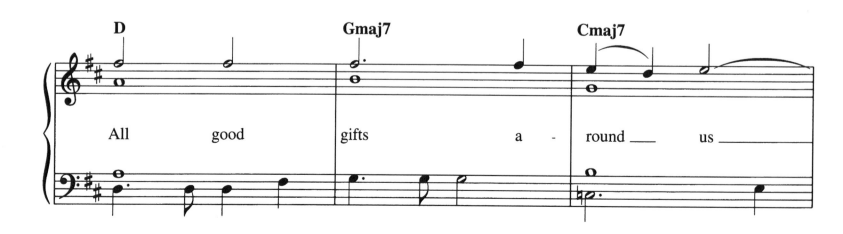

All good | gifts | a - round _ us _____

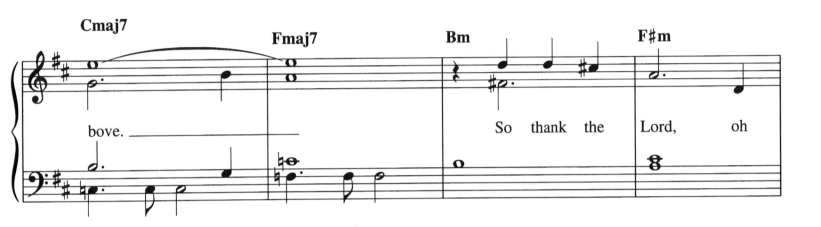

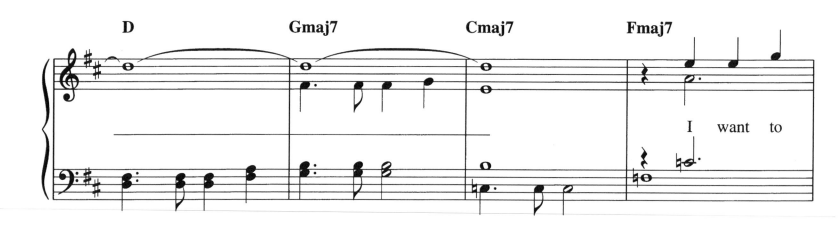

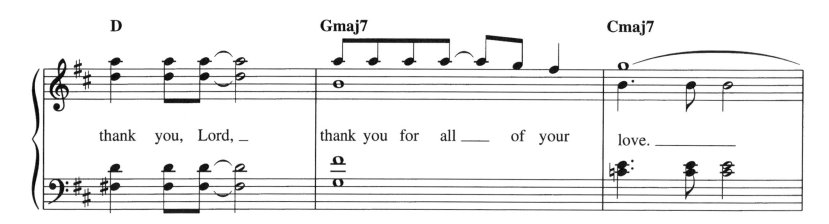

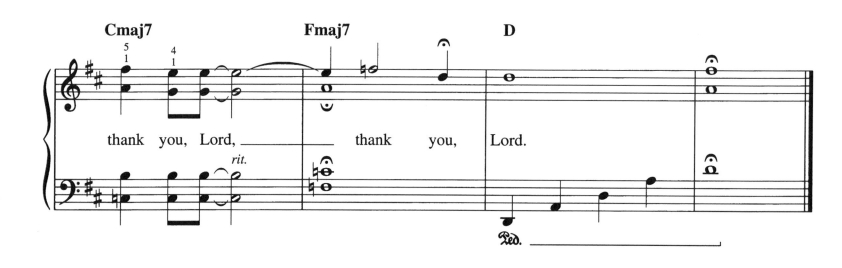

# WE BESEECH THEE

Words and Music by
STEPHEN SCHWARTZ

**Bright Hoedown**

Fa - ther hear Thy | chil-dren's call ___ | hum - bly at Thy
Sick we come to | Thee for cure ___ | guil - ty seek Thy
By the gra - cious | sav - ing call ___ | spo - ken ten - der -

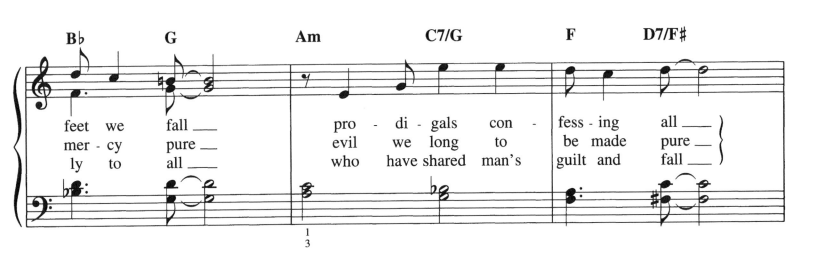

feet we fall ___ | pro - di - gals con - | fess - ing all ___
mer - cy pure ___ | evil we long to | be made pure ___
ly to all ___ | who have shared man's | guilt and fall ___

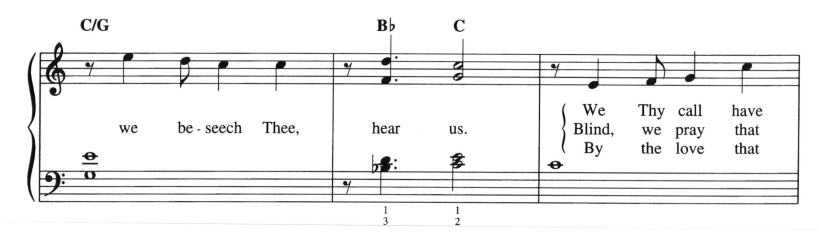

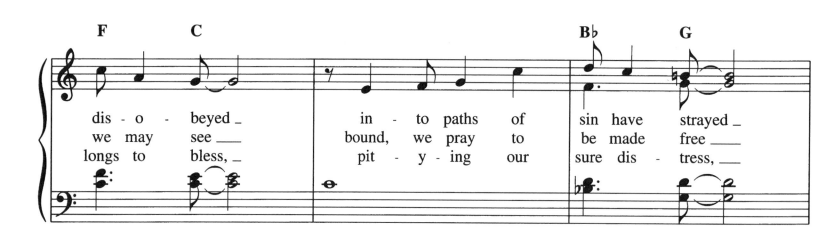

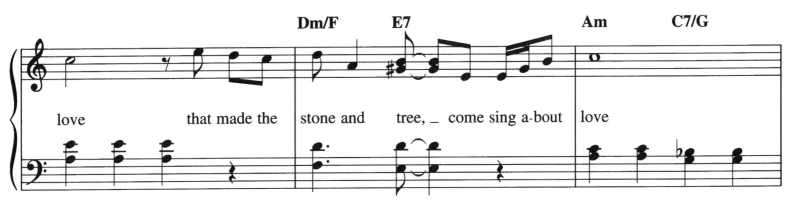

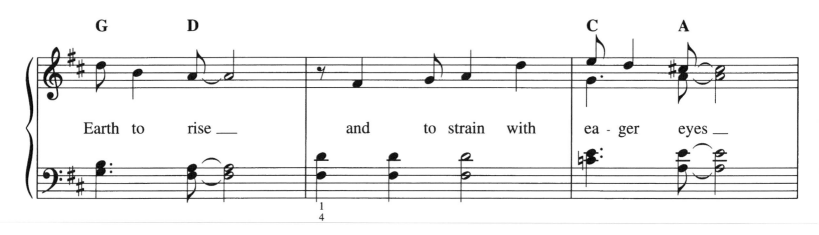

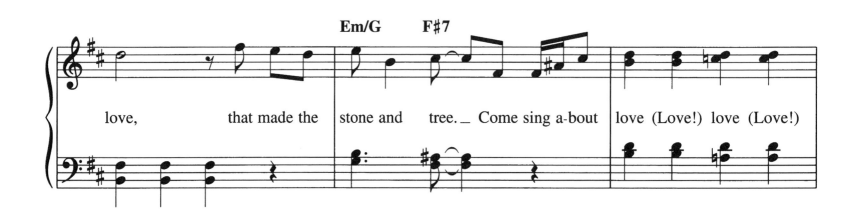

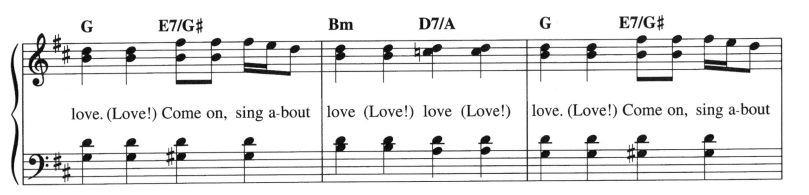

love. (Love!) Come on, sing a-bout | love (Love!) love (Love!) | love. (Love!) Come on, sing a-bout

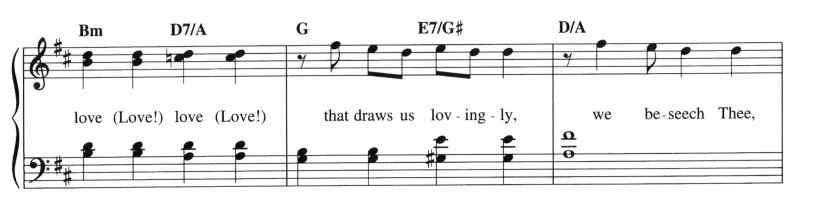

love (Love!) love (Love!) | that draws us lov-ing-ly, | we be-seech Thee,

hear us.

# TURN BACK, O MAN

Words and Music by
STEPHEN SCHWARTZ

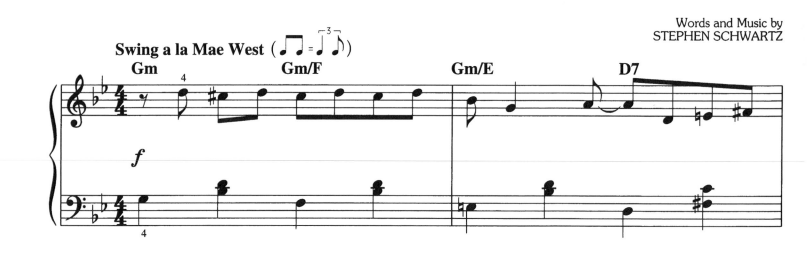

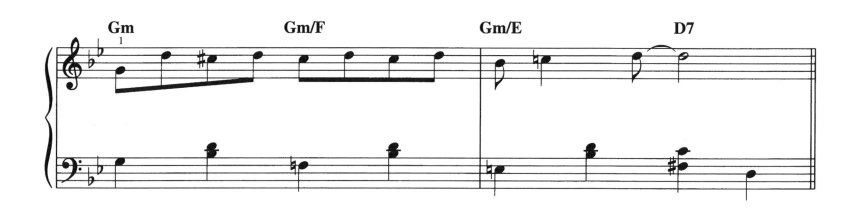

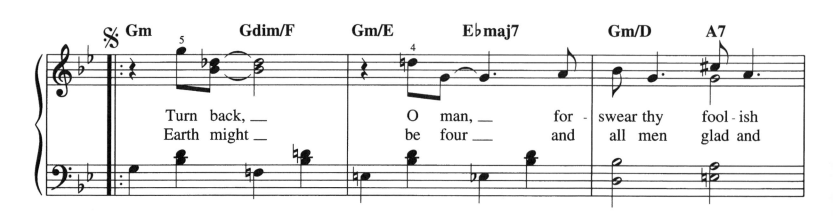

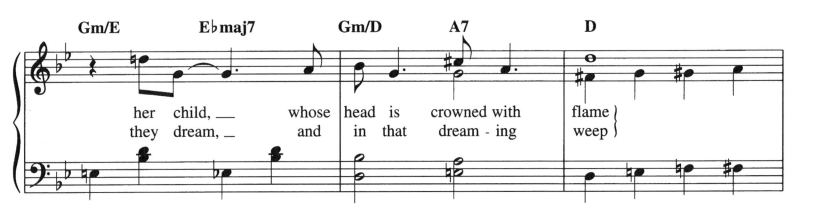

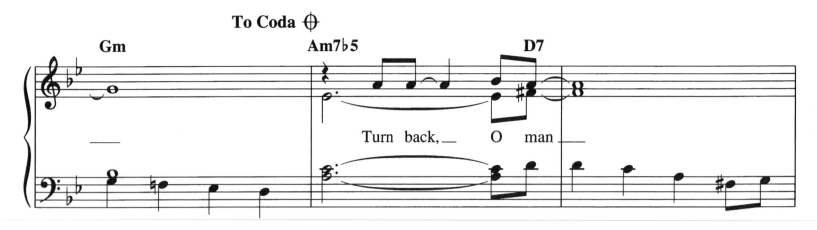

**To Coda** ⊕

Turn back,__ O man__

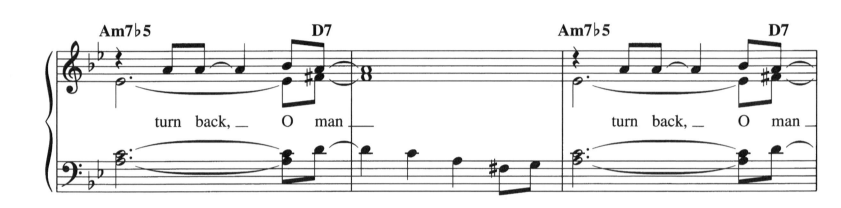

turn back,__ O man__

turn back,__ O man__

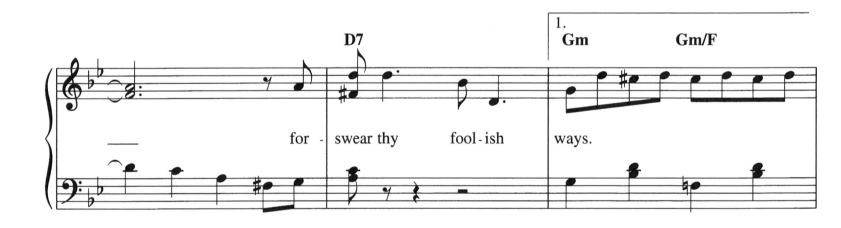

for - swear thy fool-ish ways.

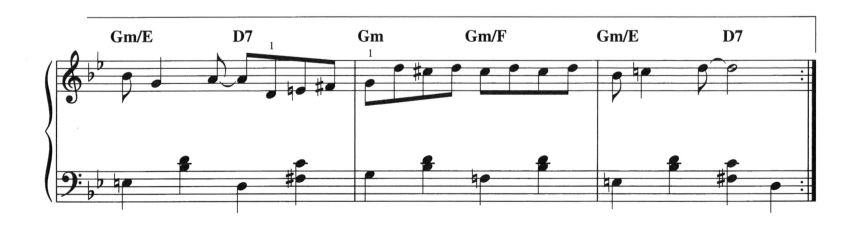

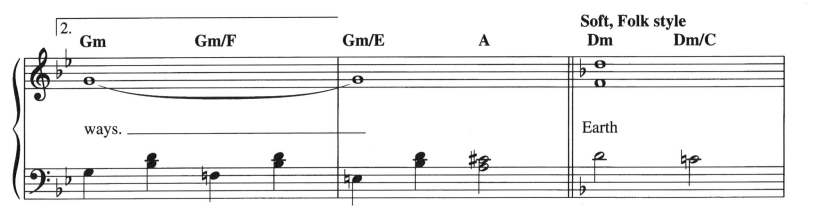

**Soft, Folk style**

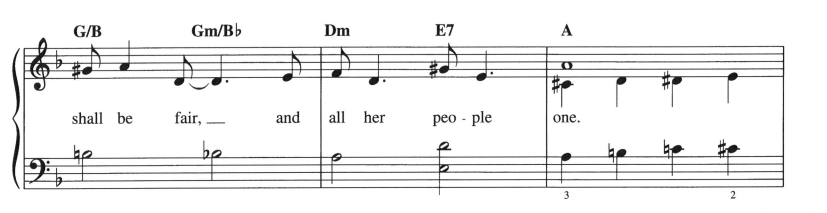

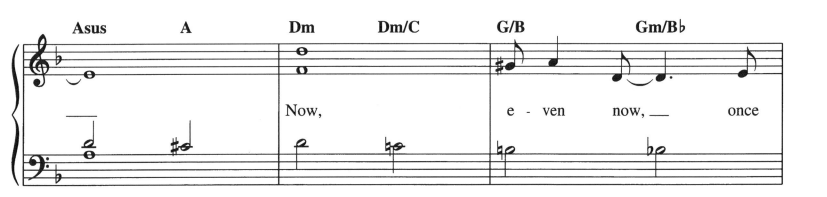

more from    earth to    sky.                    Peals   forth   in

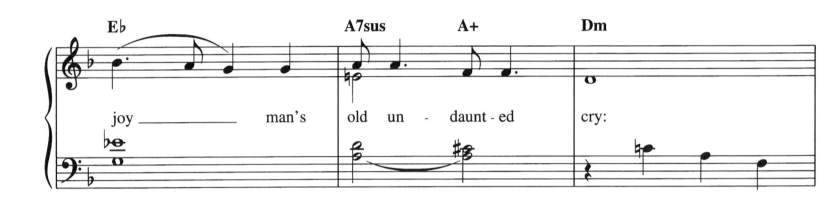

joy _____ man's   old un - daunt - ed    cry:

Earth    shall    be    fair,    and    all    her    peo - ple

**Tempo I (Mae West style)**

**D.S. al Coda**
(1st verse)

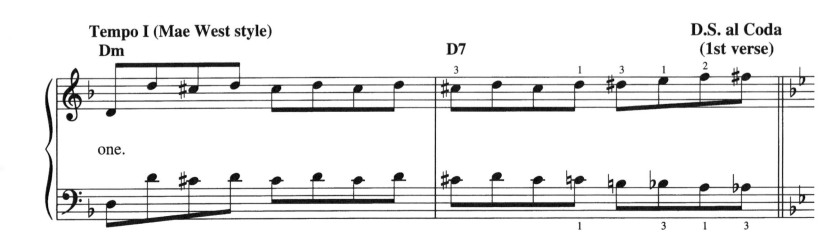

one.

**CODA**

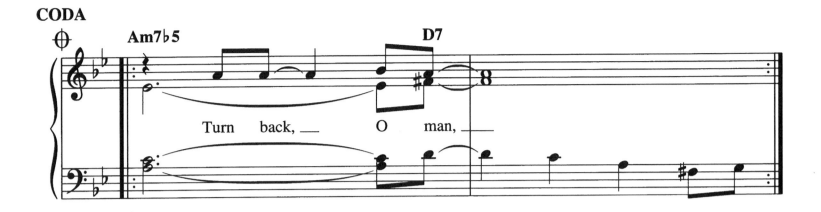

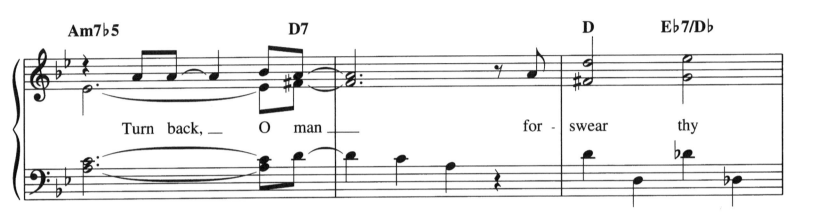

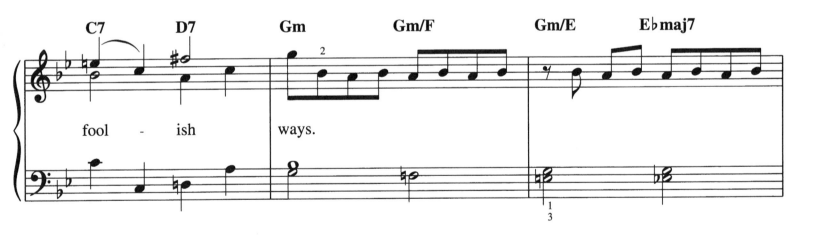

# BY MY SIDE

Words and Music by JAY HAMBURGER
and PEGGY GORDON

**Moderate folk song**

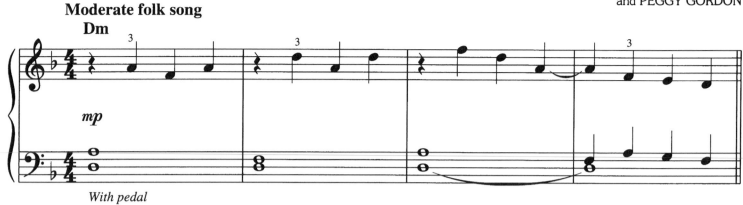

*With pedal*

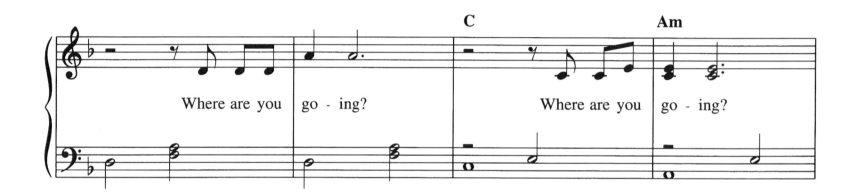

Where are you go - ing? Where are you go - ing?

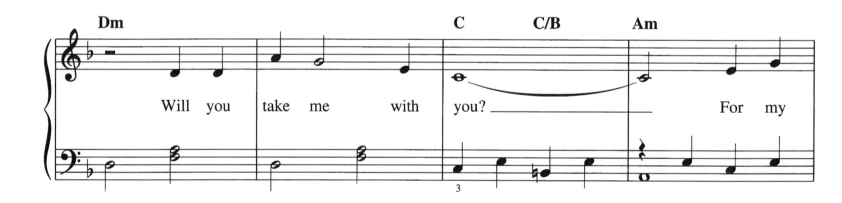

Will you take me with you? _____ For my

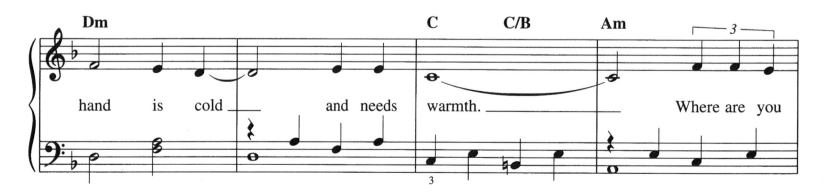

hand is cold _____ and needs warmth. _____ Where are you

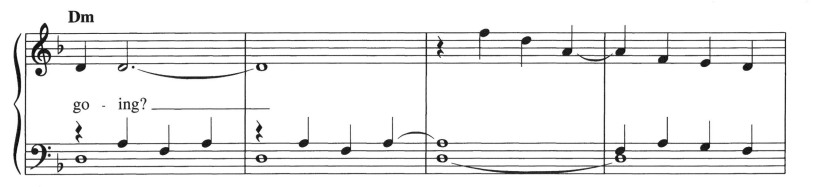

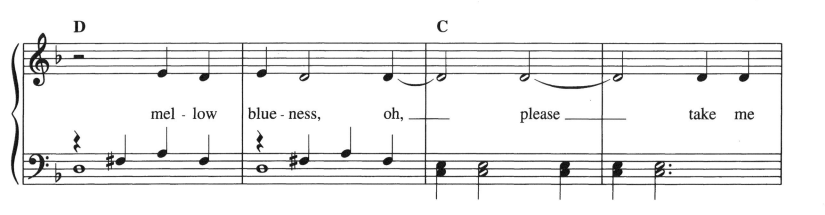

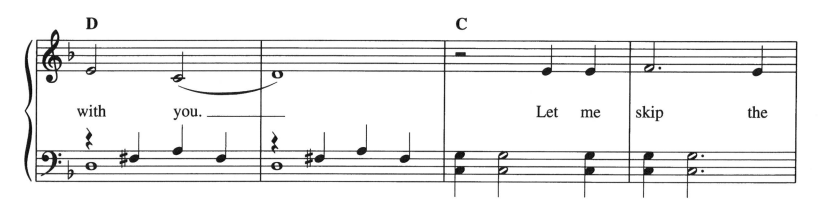

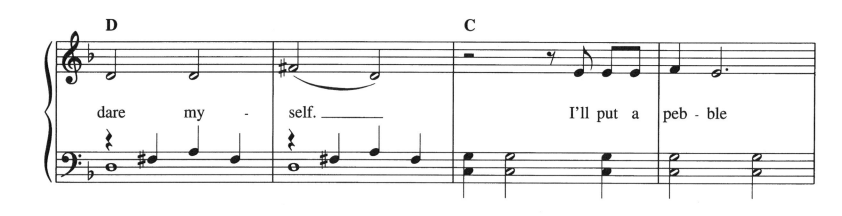

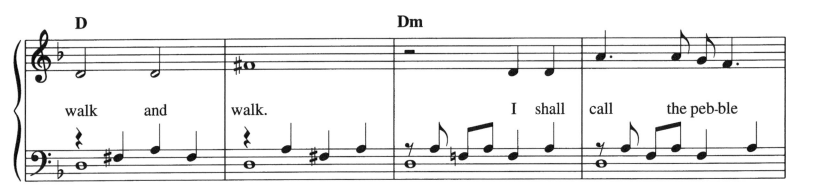

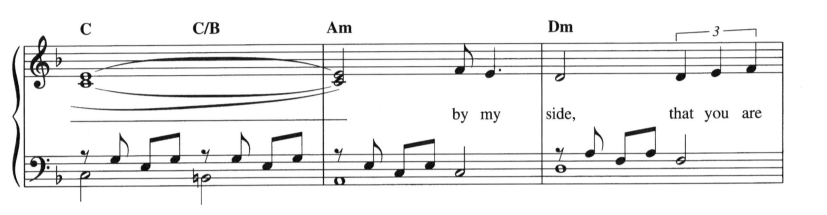

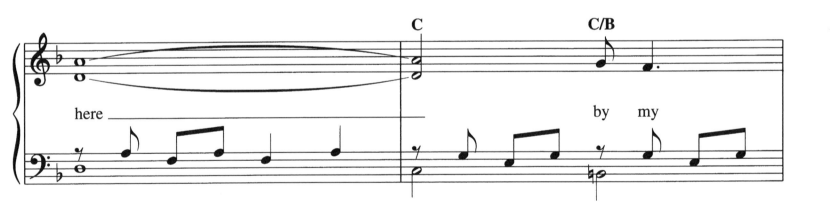

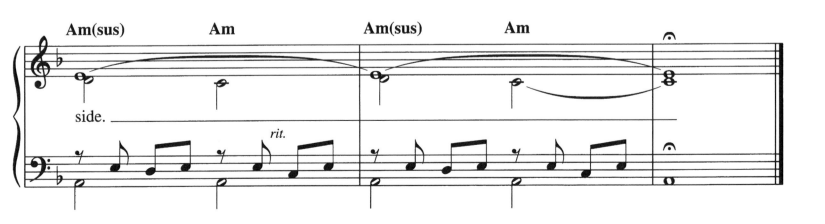

# LEARN YOUR LESSONS WELL

Words and Music by
STEPHEN SCHWARTZ

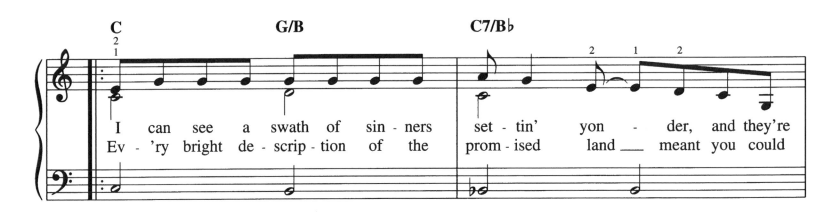

I can see a swath of sin-ners set-tin' yon-der, and they're
Ev-'ry bright de-scrip-tion of the prom-ised land ___ meant you could

act-in' like a pack of fools.
reach it if you keep a - lert.

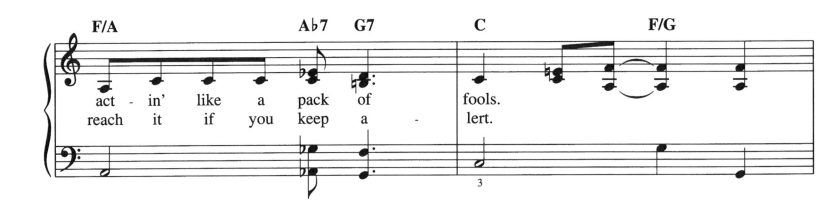

Gaz-in' in-to space, they let their minds all wan-der, 'stead of
Learn-in' ev-'ry line in ev-'ry last com-mand-ment may not

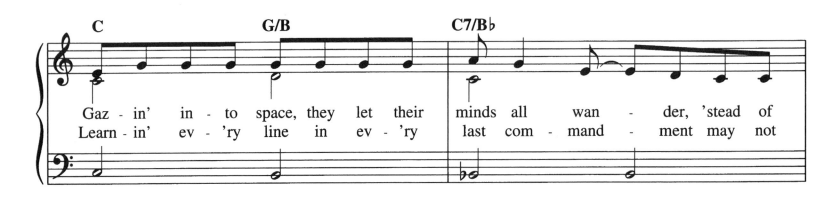

stud-y-in' the good Lord's | rules. | You | bet-ter pay at-ten-tion,
help you, but it could-n't | hurt. | | First, you got-ta read 'em,

your com-pre-hen-sion | there's gon-na be a quiz at
then you got-ta heed 'em, | you nev-er know ___ when you're

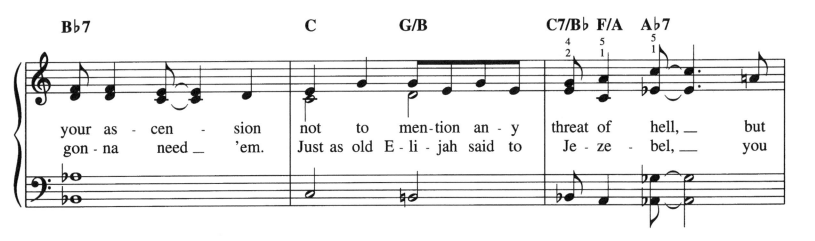

your as-cen-sion | not to men-tion an-y | threat of hell, ___ but
gon-na need ___ 'em. | Just as old E-li-jah said to | Je-ze-bel, ___ you

if you're smart, ___ you'll learn your | les-sons well. ___
bet-ter start ___ to learn your | | les-sons well. ___

# ON THE WILLOWS

Words and Music by
STEPHEN SCHWARTZ

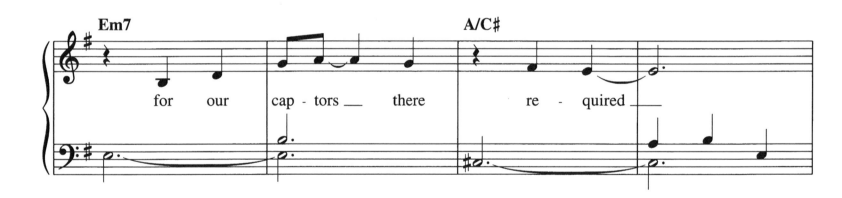

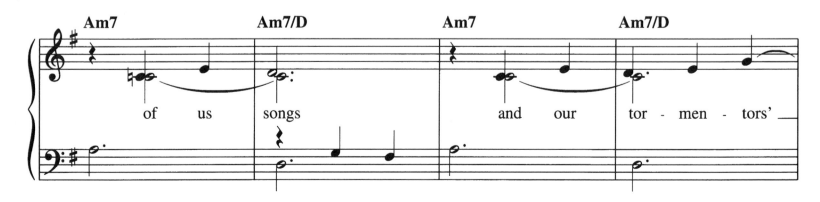

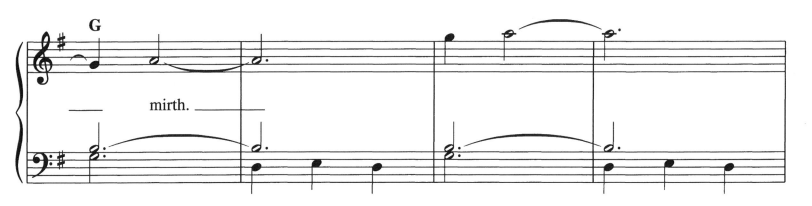

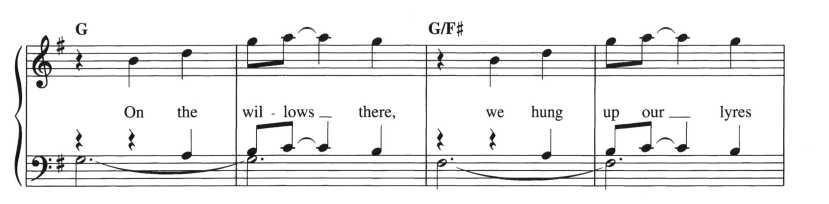

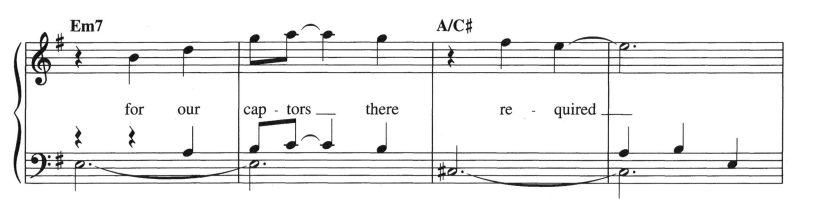

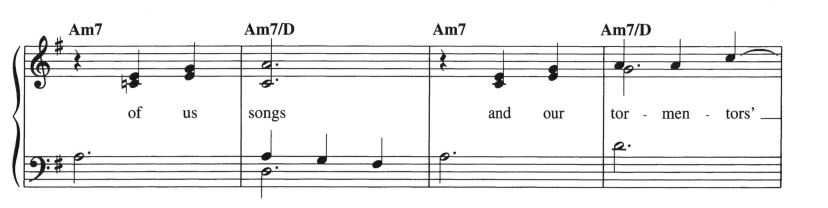

44

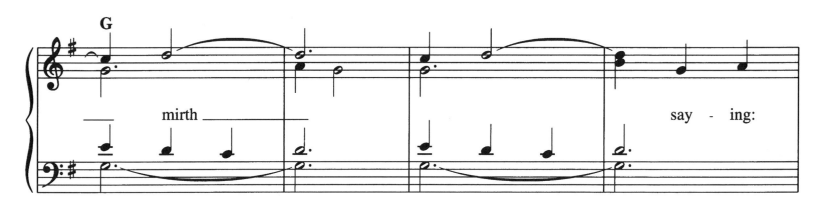

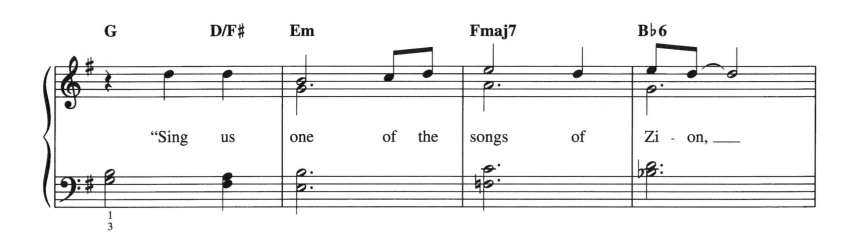

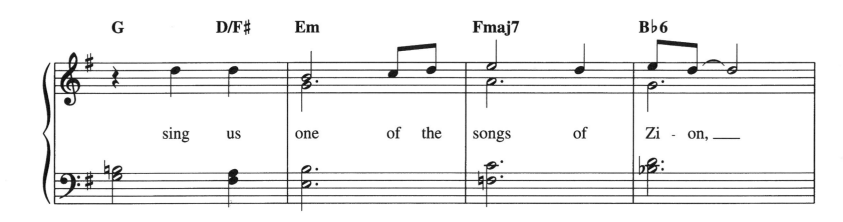

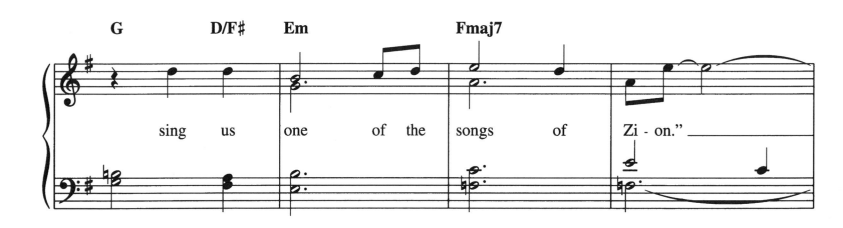

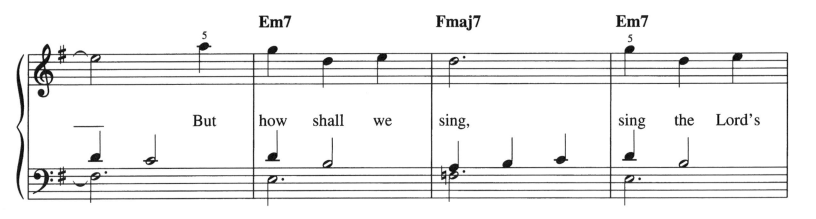

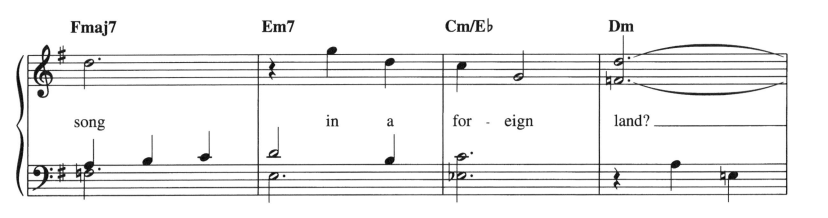

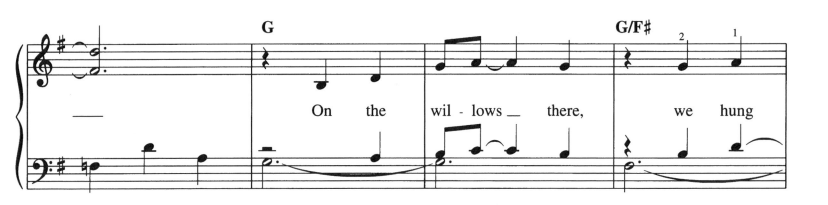

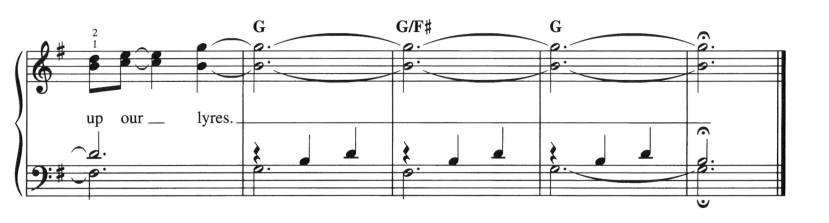

# LIGHT OF THE WORLD

Words and Music by
STEPHEN SCHWARTZ

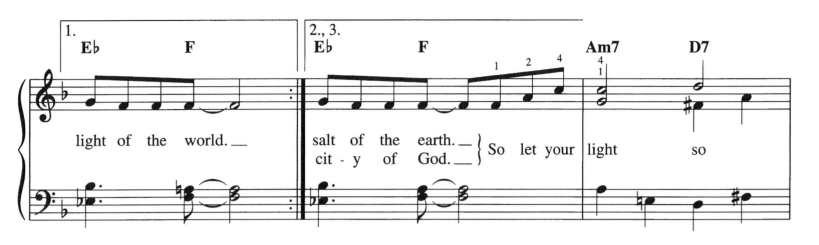

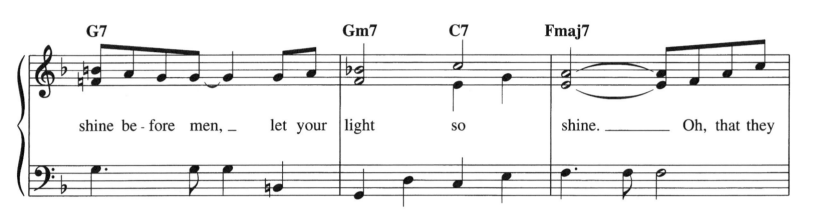

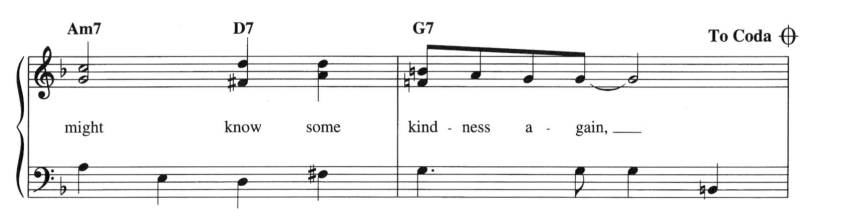

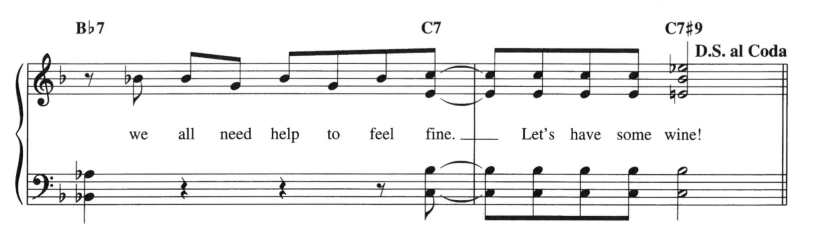

**CODA**

we all need help to feel fine.__ Let's have some wine! You are the light of the

world. You are the light of the world. But __ the

tall-est can-dle-stick _ ain't much good with-out a wick, _ you got to live right _ to be the

light of the world. _

**Repeat and Fade**